A LOOK AT THE BILL OF RIGHTS

Freedom of SPEECH

BY MARY GRIFFIN

CRASHCOURSE

Gareth Stevens PUBLISHING

Please visit our website, www.garethstevens.com. For a free color catalog of all our high-quality books, call toll free 1-800-542-2595 or fax 1-877-542-2596.

Library of Congress Cataloging-in-Publication Data
Names: Griffin, Mary, 1978- author.
Title: Freedom of speech / Mary Griffin.
Description: Buffalo : Gareth Stevens Publishing, 2026. | Series: A look at the Bill of Rights | Includes index.
Identifiers: LCCN 2024028836 | ISBN 9781482470291 (library binding) | ISBN 9781482470284 (paperback) | ISBN 9781482470307 (ebook)
Subjects: LCSH: Freedom of speech–United States–Juvenile literature. | United States. Constitution. 1st-10th amendments–Juvenile literature. | Civil rights–United States–Juvenile literature.
Classification: LCC KF4772 .G79 2026 | DDC 342.7308/53–dc23/eng/20240624
LC record available at https://lccn.loc.gov/2024028836

First Edition

Published in 2026 by
Gareth Stevens Publishing
2544 Clinton Street
Buffalo, NY 14224

Designer: Andrea Davison-Bartolotta
Editor: Kristen Rajczak Nelson

Photo credits: Cover, p. 1 Krakenimages.com/Shutterstock.com; series art (interior background texture) Nik Merkulov/Shutterstock.com; series art (fact box sticker) Sulovsky/Shutterstock.com; series art (blue backgrounds) Le Chernina/Shutterstock.com; series art (banners) saicle/Shutterstock.com; p. 4 Derek Hatfield/Shutterstock.com; p. 5 Everett Collection/Shutterstock.com; p. 7 (background) ronstik/Shutterstock.com; p. 7 (main) wingedwolf/iStockphoto.com; p. 9 Ground Picture/Shutterstock.com; p. 11 (bottom) Longfin Media/Shutterstock.com; p. 11 (top) CameraCraft/Shutterstock.com; p. 13 courtesy of Library of Congress; p. 14 File:Seal of the United States Supreme Court.svg/Wikimedia Commons; p. 15 Bob Pool/Shutterstock.com; p. 17 Shala W. Graham/Shutterstock.com; p. 19 Monkey Business Images/Shutterstock.com; p. 21 (bottom) DC Studio/Shutterstock.com; p. 21 (top) Spiroview Inc/Shutterstock.com; p. 22 Leonard Zhukovsky/Shutterstock.com; p. 23 Bart Sherkow/Shutterstock.com; p. 25 MDV Edwards/Shutterstock.com; p. 27 Richard H Grant/Shutterstock.com; p. 29 ssi77/Shutterstock.com; p. 30 Apostrophe/Shutterstock.com.

Printed in China

Some of the images in this book illustrate individuals who are models. The depictions do not imply actual situations or events.

CPSIA compliance information: Batch #QS26GS: For further information contact Gareth Stevens at 1-800-542-2595.

Contents

Words in the glossary appear in **bold** type the first time they are used in the text.

PROTECT OUR RIGHTS!

The U.S. Constitution has been in use since 1789. But it wasn't **approved** by all the states at once. Some people worried **citizens'** rights didn't have enough **protection**. So, James Madison wrote 17 amendments that listed many rights. One of these was freedom of speech!

A constitution is the basic laws that govern a country or state. An amendment is a change to a constitution.

James Madison, member of Congress from Virginia and fourth U.S. president

GUARANTEED RIGHTS

By December 1791, the states had approved 10 of the amendments. Today, these first 10 amendments to the U.S. Constitution are called the Bill of Rights. It lists rights that citizens are guaranteed, or promised, under the law.

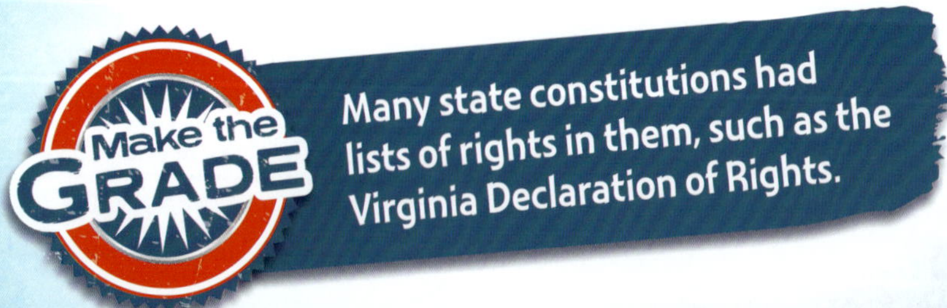

Bill of Rights

Congress OF THE United States,

began and held at the City of New York, on Wednesday, the fourth of March, one thousand seven hundred and eighty nine.

Article I...... *Congress shall make no law respecting an establishment of religion, or prohibiting the free exercise thereof; or abridging the freedom of speech, or of the press; or the right of the people peaceably to assemble, and to petition the government for a redress of grievances.*

Article II..... *A well regulated militia, being necessary to the security of a free state, the right of the people to keep and bear arms, shall not be infringed.*

Article III.... *No soldier shall, in time of peace be quartered in any house, without the consent of the owner, nor in time of war, but in a manner to be prescribed by law.*

Article IV.... *The right of the people to be secure in their persons, houses, papers, and effects, against unreasonable searches and seizures, shall not be violated, and no warrants shall issue, but upon probable cause, supported by oath or affirmation, and particularly describing the place to be searched, and the persons or things to be seized.*

Article V..... *No person shall be held to answer for a capital, or otherwise infamous crime, unless on a presentment or indictment of a grand jury, except in cases arising [illegible] land or naval forces, or in the militia, when in actual service in time of war or [illegible]ic dange[illegible] nor shall any person be subject for the same offense to be twice put in [illegible]pardy of [illegible] nor shall be compelled in any criminal case to be a witness against himse[illegible] [illegible] liberty, without due process of law; nor sha[illegible] [illegible] compensation*

PART OF THE FIRST AMENDMENT

The First Amendment of the Bill of Rights has many rights listed in it. It says in part: "Congress shall make no law . . . abridging the freedom of speech." This means the government can't make laws that take away or **weaken** citizens' right to speak.

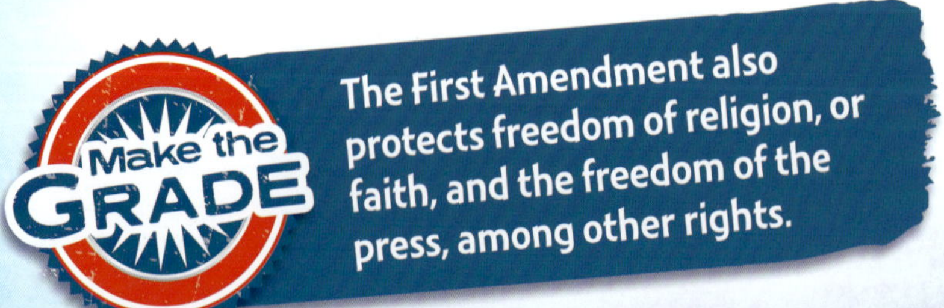

WHAT IS FREE SPEECH?

Freedom of speech means citizens can say their opinions, beliefs and ideas. The government cannot stop them, even if it doesn't agree or like what is said. Both written and spoken words are considered part of a citizens' right to free speech.

Symbolic speech is part of free speech. It has to do with actions, such as the clothes a person wears, what a person reads, and even what they may protest, or speak out in favor or against.

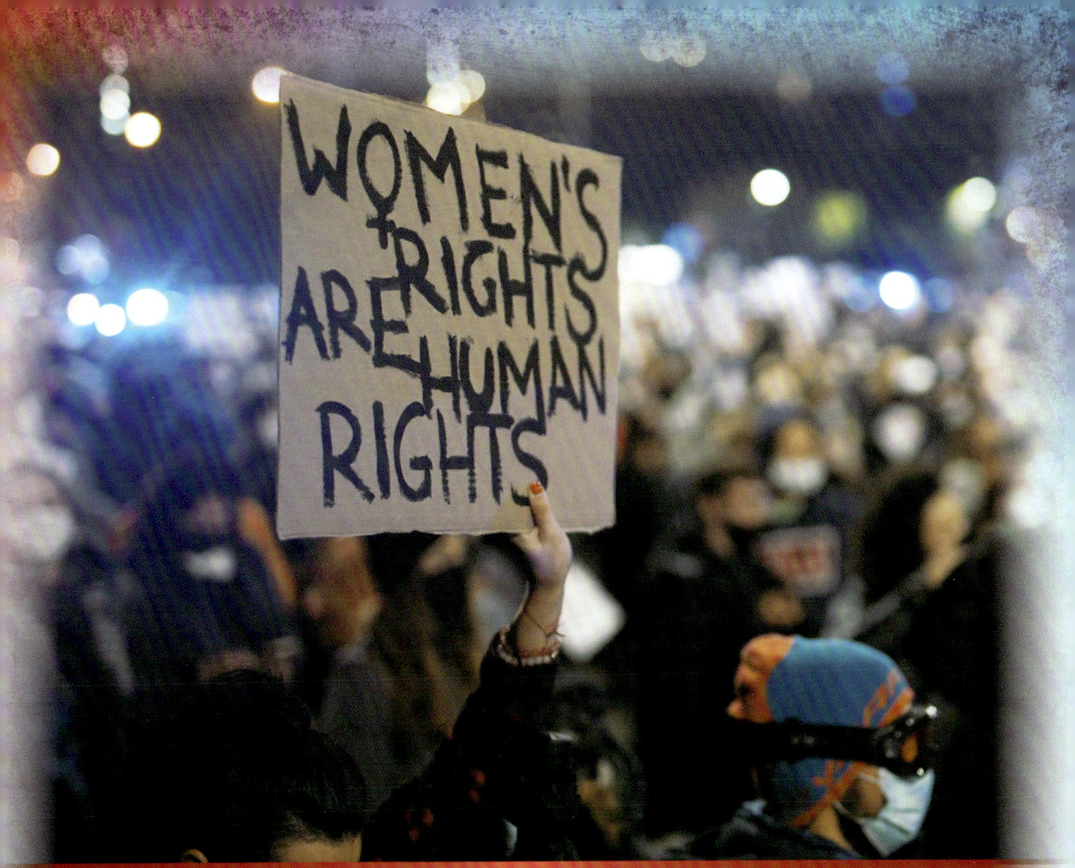
WOMEN'S
RIGHTS
ARE HUMAN
RIGHTS

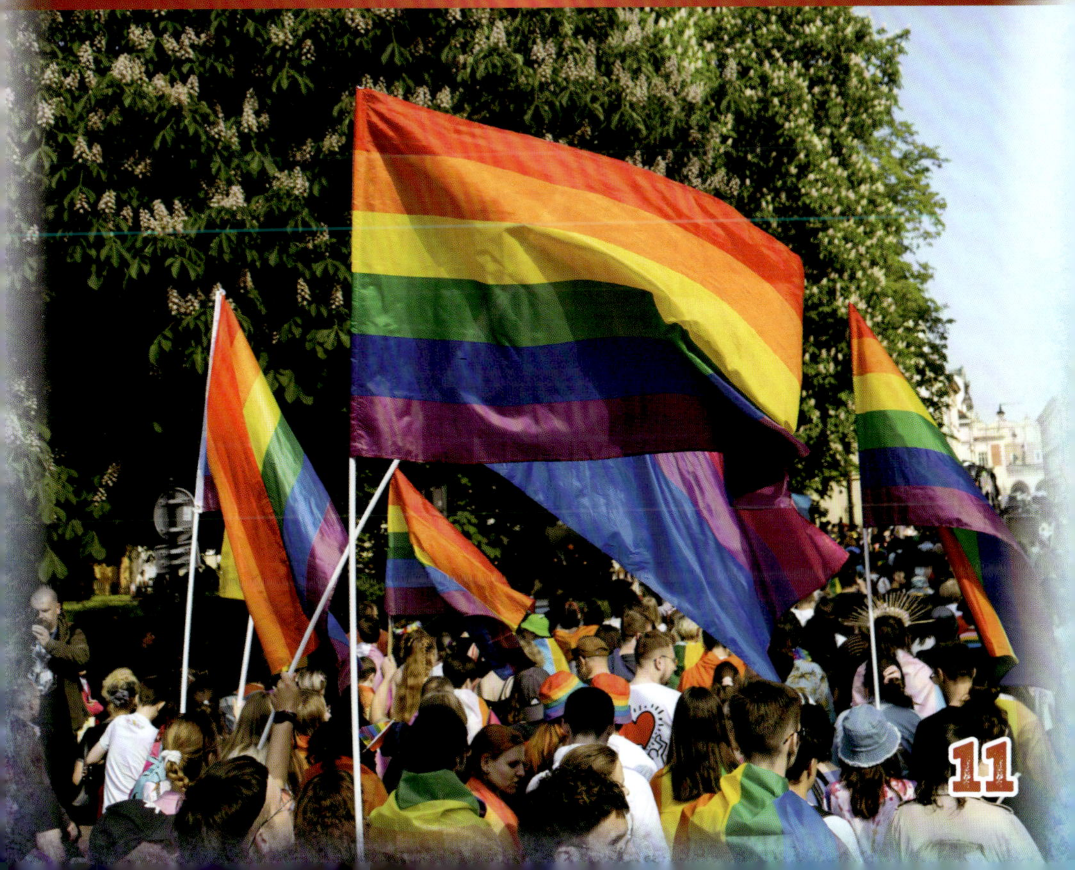

WHY INCLUDE IT?

The first 13 U.S. states started out as English **colonies**. It was against the law for them to speak out against the government. Adding freedom of speech to the Bill of Rights meant citizens could share their opinions about the government without fear of being **punished**.

King George III was king of England when the U.S. colonies **declared** their freedom.

THE ROLE OF THE COURT

Freedom of speech may seem simple. But, the highest court in the United States, the Supreme Court, has been figuring it out for hundreds of years! It decides whether laws and actions of citizens and the government are constitutional, or follow the Constitution.

Make the GRADE

The Supreme Court has heard hundreds of cases about freedom of speech. Lawmakers look to the court's decisions to guide them in making laws.

PROTECTED SPEECH

Protected speech is spoken, written, and symbolic speech allowed by law or Supreme Court ruling. The court protects freedom of speech if what was said or expressed is based in fact or an opinion truly held by a citizen or group.

A citizen or group may **express** opinions other people find hateful, mean, or **racist**. This is often protected speech. The reason for this is so all sides of an issue may be heard by the public.

WE
are the
MAJORITY
HEAR OUR
VOICES

In *Tinker v. Des Moines* in 1968, the Supreme Court decided students have the constitutional right to free speech in school. A school tried to stop students from wearing black armbands to protest the Vietnam War during the 1960s. The court sided with the students!

Make the GRADE
Not every Supreme Court decision is unanimous, or agreed on by all the justices serving on the court.

In 1943, the Supreme Court decided in *West Virginia Board of Education v. Barnette* that citizens could not be forced to **salute** the American flag. It would **violate** their First Amendment rights to freedom of speech—in this case, their right not to speak or act.

Make the GRADE

Freedom of expression is part of freedom of speech. This includes making music and art, even cartoons.

The Supreme Court decided in 1988 that parody is protected speech. Parody is writing, art, or music that copies the work of someone else in an amusing, or funny, way. The TV show *Saturday Night Live* often uses parody, as does the music artist "Weird Al" Yankovic.

"Weird Al" Yankovic

Make the GRADE

Sometimes parody is simply meant to be funny. Sometimes it is used to send a message or point something out about a person, group, news story, or the government.

CAUSING HARM

Certain kinds of speech are not protected under the First Amendment as **interpreted** by the Supreme Court. People can't incite, or try to cause, others to break the law. Threats of violence, or harm, to others aren't protected speech. **Harassment** isn't protected either.

Defamation is when something untrue is said or written about another person and it caused that person harm. It is not simply giving an opinion. This is not protected speech.

GOVERNMENT WORKERS

Government workers have less free speech rights at times. They may be punished for something they said on the job. This is meant to keep the government running smoothly and safely. Supreme Court cases have shaped when government workers have First Amendment protection and when they don't.

Make the GRADE

The 14th Amendment made the protections of the Bill of Rights apply to state governments too.

FREE SPEECH ONLINE

The Supreme Court hears many cases about freedom of speech. In 2024, it heard cases about how this First Amendment right applies to speech on the internet and social media. This is a new area of freedom of speech. The court's decisions will matter for years to come!

Social media are websites and applications, also known as apps, used to create online communities. Facebook, Instagram, TikTok, YouTube, and X are all part of social media.

WHAT SPEECH IS PROTECTED?

protected speech

- symbolic speech
- not speaking or acting
- opinion
- comments about the government
- art
- parody

not protected speech

- threats
- harassment
- defamation
- inciting others to break the law
- some types of speech by government workers on the job

These are just some forms of protected and unprotected speech. There are many more!

Glossary

approve: To give official agreement.

citizen: Someone who lives in a country legally and has certain rights.

colony: A piece of land under the control of another country.

declare: To officially state.

express: To make known.

harassment: To do something over and over that bothers and harms another person.

interpret: To tell the meaning of.

protection: The state of being kept safe.

punish: To make someone suffer for wrongdoing, such as through jail time or a fine.

racist: The belief that some races of people are better than others.

salute: To show a sign of respect, often by putting the hand to the forehead.

violate: To do something that is not allowed by law.

weaken: To make less strong.

For More Information

Books

Matulli, Allison, and Clelia Castro-Malaspina. *Your Freedom, Your Power: A Kid's Guide to the First Amendment.* Philadelphia, PA: Running Press Kids, 2023.

Keppeler, Jill. *What Is the First Amendment?* Buffalo, NY: Rosen Publishing, 2023.

Website

Bill of Rights
https://bensguide.gpo.gov/bill-of-rights-1789-91
Check out this short guide to all the amendments included in the Bill of Rights.

Index